I0605229

PRACTICAL CAREERS FOR PRACTICAL PEOPLE

PLUMBER

Cathleen Small

Published in 2026 by **Cheriton Children's Books**
1 Bank Drive West, Shrewsbury, Shropshire, SY3 9DJ, UK

First Edition

Author: Cathleen Small
Designer: Jessica Moon
Editor: Sarah Eason
Proofreader: Amy Strauss

Picture credits: Cover: Shutterstock/Monkey Business Images. Inside: p3: Shutterstock/Noomcpk, p4: Shutterstock/BAZA Production, p5: Shutterstock/Alpa Prod, p6: Shutterstock/Anatoliy Gleb, p7: Shutterstock/Monkey Business Images, p8: Shutterstock/Pixel Shot, p9: Shutterstock/Dragon Images, p10: Shutterstock/Sashko, p11: Shutterstock/Andrey Popov, p12: Shutterstock/Pixel Shot, p13: Shutterstock/PeopleImages.com/Yuri A, p14: Shutterstock/Alpa Prod, p17: Shutterstock/Monkey Business Images, p18: Shutterstock/Monkey Business Images, p19: Shutterstock/Monkey Business Images, p20: Shutterstock/Roman Zaiets, p21: Shutterstock/Monkey Business Images, p22: Shutterstock/Alpa Prod, p23: Shutterstock/Andrew Angelov, p24: Shutterstock/Andrey Popov, p25: Shutterstock/Pics721, p26: Shutterstock/Steklo, p27: Shutterstock/Amorn Suriyan, p28: Shutterstock/MMD Creative, p29: Shutterstock/Virrage Images, p30: Shutterstock/Tong Stocker, p33l: Shutterstock/August 0802, p33r: Shutterstock/Mangkorn Danggura, p34: Shutterstock/Viktor LA, p35: Shutterstock/A Lot Of People, p36: Shutterstock/Maksim Safaniuk, p37: Shutterstock/AY Amazefoto, p38: Shutterstock/Pakulin Sergei, p39: Shutterstock/Hryshchyshen Serhii, p40: Shutterstock/Michael Zimzim, p41: Shutterstock/Pressmaster, p42: Shutterstock/Krakenimages.com, p43: Shutterstock/AJR Photo, p44: Shutterstock/Skylines, p47: Shutterstock/Alpa Prod, p48: Shutterstock/Michael Vi, p49: Shutterstock/Eakarat Buanoi, p50: Shutterstock/Andrew Angelov, p51: Shutterstock/Davizro Photography, p53: Shutterstock/Phovoir, p54: Shutterstock/Hryshchyshen Serhii, p55: Shutterstock/APChanel, p57b: Shutterstock, p57t: Shutterstock/Frame Stock Footage, p63: Shutterstock/Monkey Business Images.

Printed in China

Please visit our website,
www.cheritonchildrensbooks.com
to see more of our high-quality books.

CONTENTS

CHAPTER 1

Working in the Plumbing Industry

When you talk to your friends and peers, it might seem that everyone you know is planning on going to college. The US Census Bureau states that more than 37 percent of people aged 25 and older have at least a bachelor's degree—and obviously there are some people who attend college but haven't completed a degree by the time they are 25. That means a lot of people are going to college now. But it also means there are many people who aren't. Maybe you're one of the number who does not want to go. If so, we've got good news for you!

GOOD NEWS FOR PRACTICAL PEOPLE

Practical careers are a great option for students who prefer hands-on work that doesn't involve sitting behind a desk. In fact, qualified people for practical careers are in more demand than ever because so many people are choosing to go to

If your future plans don't seem to be pointing toward college, there's good news because people skilled in practical careers are in high demand.

Every building and residence requires plumbing. Plumbers are in great demand as a result.

college and pursue the jobs associated with college degrees. If you're a person who likes the satisfaction that comes from solving problems and working with your hands, that's great news.

A DEMAND FOR PLUMBERS

Plumbing is a practical line of work that is in high demand. Every single house, apartment, condo, or office building requires plumbing. And public areas and facilities require plumbing, too. Think about local parks. They require irrigation, which is typically handled by landscapers. But they also have bathroom facilities, drinking fountains, and the like, which all need to be installed and maintained by plumbers. And if the park has a sprayground area, as many do in hotter parts of the United States, plumbing is required there, too.

Needless to say, there will always be a need for qualified plumbers. If you choose to go into plumbing as a career, you'll have many areas in which you can choose to work.

THINKING ABOUT WORKING IN THE PLUMBING INDUSTRY

When you're thinking about your future plumbing career, there are several factors to consider:

- Do you have skills in the plumbing field—or could you develop them?
- Will the job be secure?
- Will the job likely exist in the future as technology advances and introduces changes to the workplace?
- How much will you earn?
- What training is involved, and how much will it cost?
- What benefits does the plumbing field offer in addition to pay?

We'll explore the answers to all the above questions in this chapter.

IN IT FOR THE LONG TERM

Currently, the average American male retires at age 65, and the average American woman retires at age 62, according to the Center for Retirement Research at Boston College. This means that people of your generation will likely be working for a long time. So it's important to choose your career carefully—you will probably be doing it for many years to come.

THINKING AHEAD

You may only have just begun to think seriously about your career. And you've probably realized that you'll likely be working for more than 40 years, depending on when you retire. That means your career should be something you enjoy. While it has been said that money can't buy happiness—and that's true—pay is definitely a big consideration when thinking about your career. But even more important is finding a career you think you'll find satisfying.

You can, of course, change careers later in your life if you decide you don't like what you're doing. But it's not always easy to make big changes in your working life, so it's good that you're exploring career options now. At this age, you have some time to narrow down what you think you might enjoy doing for the coming decades.

WOULD YOU ENJOY BEING A PLUMBER?

So let's talk about whether you'd like being a plumber. One great aspect about being a plumber is the variety of work the job involves. There are all sorts of reasons why people need plumbers. That means no two workdays are the same because no two problems and solutions to them are identical. So, if you like change and variety, you'll enjoy being a plumber.

You also get a lot of personal interaction as a plumber. Whether you're going into people's homes on service calls or installing plumbing in a series of new homes along with a team of other contractors, there will always be people around. If you're someone who enjoys interacting with others, that's a big plus.

When thinking about a career in plumbing, ask yourself whether you'd enjoy it. Job satisfaction is the most important piece of the puzzle when you're figuring out what you want to do.

Residential plumbing is just one part of the field. There are plenty of opportunities in this section of the industry.

FAMOUS PLUMBERS

You might not think there could be famous plumbers, but indeed there are! In the sixteenth century, Sir John Harrington of England designed the flushing toilet and installed one in his home. That revolutionized indoor plumbing (not to mention sanitation).

And if you decide to do repair work you'll certainly be appreciated. Any homeowner will be pleased to see you if they are having issues with their plumbing systems.

In addition, there are opportunities to work independently. You can work for an established company, but you can also set up your own plumbing company and be your own boss, if you prefer. And finally, plumbers make good money. It's a skilled trade in high demand, and the pay reflects that.

EARN AS YOU LEARN

"One of the best things about being a plumber is that you get to learn on the job. You don't need a four-year degree, so this a great career option if you want to start working and earning right away."

DO YOU HAVE THE RIGHT SKILLS?

Maybe you've found an interest in plumbing because someone in your family was a plumber, and you grew up learning about the industry. Or maybe you're interested in the job, but you've never tried plumbing in your life. Either way, you may have the skills it takes to be a plumber. Many of the skills you need are transferable from other areas. For example, have you ever played with building sets? Did you need to connect various parts together to move an object from one area to another (such as a marble maze)? If so, you've developed the skill to envision what is needed to move an object from one place to another. That's exactly what a plumber who is piping a new home needs to do. And if you've ever studied designs or diagrams of buildings, you've developed the skills needed to read blueprints. Does that mean you're ready to launch a career in plumbing? Not yet. But it does mean you have a head start on developing the skills you'll need.

Learning plumbing skills is empowering.

SUCCESS STORIES

While plumbers earn a good salary, most people think that plumbers are not big earners. But earning a lot of money as a plumber is possible. Charlie Mullins, a British plumber, started skipping school when he was nine years old to help a local plumber. He learned on the job and eventually founded a company, Pimlico Plumbers, which became London's largest independent plumbing company. In 2021, he sold most of the company for more than $160 million! (His son retained a small interest in the company and is an executive in it.)

Now, we don't advocate skipping school, despite Charlie's success. As you'll learn in this book, almost every career in the plumbing industry will require you to have a high school diploma or GED. So stay in school and keep learning. Then go out and build a solid career in plumbing—and maybe a big business too!

IS THERE JOB SECURITY?

Job security is an important consideration when planning your future career. You want to make sure your job will still be around in 20, 30, or 40 years, after all. The good news is the outlook for plumbers is strong. According to the Bureau of Labor Statistics (BLS), job growth for plumbers is 2 percent over the next decade. That might sound like a small amount, but it's about the average pace for jobs in the United States. And the key is that it's growth, not decline. As we'll discuss later in the book, artificial intelligence (AI) is impacting many job fields and resulting in a decline in jobs in some. However, currently that is not the case with plumbers—and it's not a career that is likely to be impacted by AI in the future.

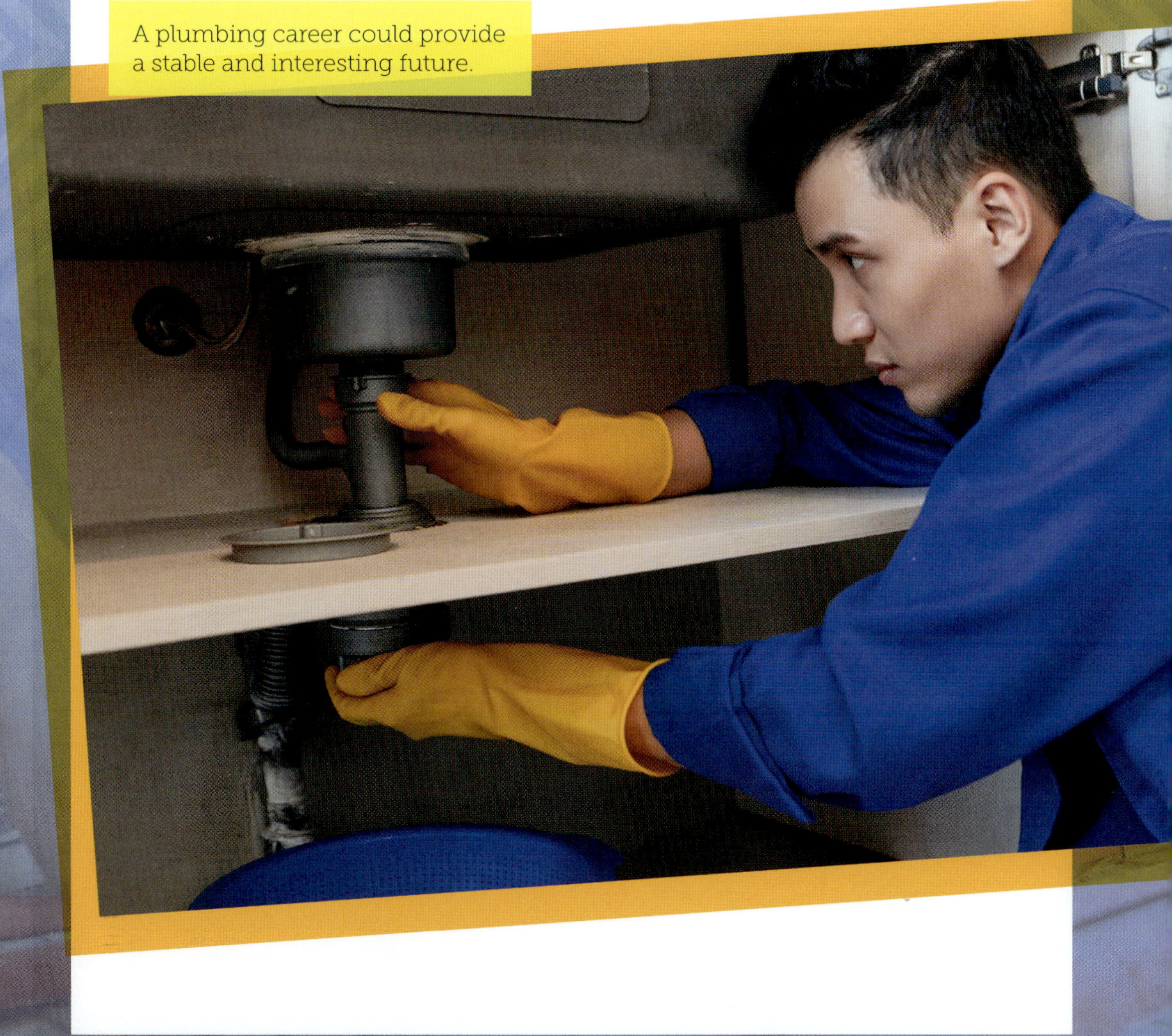

A plumbing career could provide a stable and interesting future.

WHAT WILL THE FUTURE BRING?

The biggest change to all industries these days is likely to be AI. There are fears that AI and robots are replacing human workers, costing people jobs. Some people worry about the end of the American workforce as we know it. Other people embrace AI and look forward to seeing where it takes us in the future. The good news is, in the plumbing industry AI is largely seen as a positive. AI tools can help plumbers do their job better, but they aren't replacing plumbers.

YOU'LL ALWAYS HAVE A JOB

"I've never been out of work since becoming a plumber. Plumbers are always in high demand."

GOING GREEN: AI, PLUMBING, AND THE ENVIRONMENT

One thing that might surprise you about AI and plumbing is how it's helping to contribute to more sustainable practices in the industry. Water conservation is an important issue, especially in parts of the world that frequently suffer from drought conditions, such as the American West. AI is being used to monitor and optimize water usage, reducing excess water waste. For example, some new-build homes are equipped with a small device that collects rainwater. AI then communicates to the home's sprinkler and irrigation system that there is no need to run sprinklers or drip lines when a sufficient amount of water has come from recent rain.

You might think water conservation would limit the need for plumbers, but the opposite is true. Water-smart solutions have opened up plenty of opportunities for plumbing professionals.

In any industry, there is the question of whether AI is going to take away jobs. However, the plumbing industry will always need skilled plumbers. AI can simply help them work more efficiently.

Realistically, AI and robots cannot replace plumbers. There are simply far too many unique situations that can arise in the plumbing sector. Imagine a burst water main in a road—AI isn't going to be able to fix that, nor will a robot. There are too many steps involved. However, AI is being used for some areas, such as detecting leaks. It can then alert people about them so that they know it's time to call a plumber—before the leak becomes serious. That's good news for homeowners, but it's also good news for plumbers. Leak detection helps them know exactly where the problem is, so diagnosing the problem takes less time. And fixing a leak takes a lot less time than fixing a pipe that has burst and destroyed the subfloor under a bathtub, for example. Early detection of problems means a plumber can fix them quickly and move on to the next job. And increasing the number of customers a plumber can see quickly means they can complete more jobs and earn more money.

In addition, AI is used for inventory management. That ensures that plumbers spend less time taking inventory of parts and that they always have the tools and parts they need to do their job. AI is also being used to drive virtual reality (VR) systems that help train new plumbers. They can learn to work on a variety of plumbing issues through these virtual simulations.

The average pay for plumbers is above the national average. If you have the skills needed to be a good plumber, that's great news for you!

HOW MUCH WILL I EARN?

So far, the job sounds excellent, right? But we haven't yet discussed an issue of great importance to most people: pay. According to the BLS, the median income for plumbers, pipefitters, and steamfitters is about $61,550. The top 10 percent, however, earn more than $100,000.

Your pay will depend on a lot of factors, including experience, who you work for, and where you're working. A plumber in a tiny town in the Heartland, for example, is likely to earn less than a plumber in a high-priced city such as New York or San Francisco. In fact, websites such as Salary.com, Glassdoor.com, and ZipRecruiter.com report that the average salary for a plumber in San Francisco is anywhere from just under $70,000 per year to above $115,000 per year. That is well above that median income reported by the BLS. Keep that in mind when you think about your future earnings. The takeaway is that the pay is good and will ultimately be determined by where you live, who you work for, and your skills and training.

IS IT THE RIGHT JOB FOR YOU?

So is plumbing the right job for you? There are certain skills and abilities you'll need to have if you want to succeed as a plumber:

- **Problem-solving:** Plumbers need to be able to troubleshoot and problem-solve. That applies whether they're working on fixing problems in customers' homes or piping a new office building.
- **Analytical thinking:** Plumbers need to think logically to be able to problem-solve effectively. There's certainly room for creative thinking, as some problems require creative solutions. But by and large, plumbers are analytical, logical thinkers who look at an issue and determine a logical way to solve it.
- **Good coordination:** Plumbers need to work with small parts at times, and you'll need good hand-eye coordination to be able to fit those small parts and use tools in very small spaces, sometimes.
- **Good with people:** Plumbers spend much of their time working with people. You may be working with a team of other contractors, or you may be meeting people in their home or office to diagnose and solve a problem. Either way, being good with people goes a long way in establishing your reputation as a plumber. If you do a good job and people like you, they'll want to call you again when they have a job or problem that needs solving.

(See page 21 for more key attributes.)

GREAT FOR PRACTICAL PEOPLE

"Not everyone is academic —I never was. But I've loved learning in this job. You get to find out how to do things in a hands-on way, and that suits me."

If you have the type of brain that enjoys getting to the root of a problem and fixing it, you'd find plumbing a satisfying career.

LOOKING AT SALARIES AND COSTS OF COLLEGE

As you have learned, the salary for plumbers is attractive. One thing that's also helpful is weighing the salary expectations for plumbing work against the cost of going to college. Plumbing doesn't require a four-year college degree. Instead, there are a few training paths you can follow, and none of them is as expensive as going to college for four years. You can attend a trade school, or you can explore apprenticeship options, some of which are offered in conjunction with community colleges. Either way, the cost of your training is going to be far less than the cost of a four-year degree.

According to the Education Data Initiative (EDI), the average cost of a four-year college education at an in-state public university in the United States is at least $108,000. The average cost of a four-year college education at an out-of-state university is more than $182,000. The average cost of a four-year college education at a private university is more than $234,000. The initiative also reports that the average borrower of student loans spends 20 years paying them off.

HOW MUCH WILL I NEED TO TRAIN AND WHAT WILL IT COST?

The cost of plumbing schools varies widely but tends to be anywhere from $1,000 to just under $30,000, depending on where you go. Even though that is a huge range, the highest figure is still far less than the cost of college. In some cases, it is far less than the cost of even just one year of college. So that's something to consider. Spending six figures on a college education is sensible if you have a career you'll love in mind, and it requires that outlay. But if you think a practical career such as plumbing is far more your speed, then a major benefit is that you won't have to go into a lot of debt to accomplish your schooling. Less debt means more of your hard-earned money stays in your pocket instead of paying off student loans. And that still applies if you decide to attend a trade school. Another option is to do an apprenticeship, which will cost you even less. (We'll discuss training in further detail in Chapter 2.)

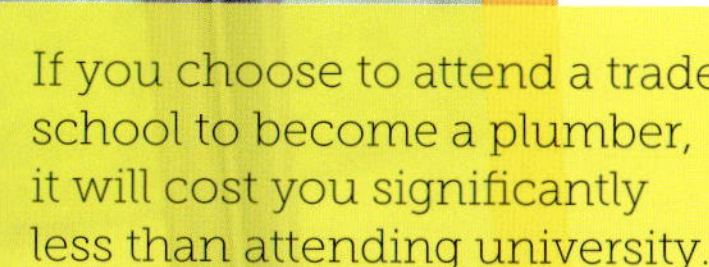

If you choose to attend a trade school to become a plumber, it will cost you significantly less than attending university.

WHAT OTHER BENEFITS ARE THERE?

When it comes to choosing a career, pay isn't everything. It's important to consider the total compensation package that comes with a job. Total compensation typically includes your salary, any insurance offerings (such as health and life), and any retirement plans.

What your total compensation package includes depends highly on your employer and whether you are self-employed or employed by a company. If you're self-employed, it will be your responsibility to acquire insurance and set up a retirement plan. If you're employed by a company, your employer may or may not provide these. However, either way, most plumbers belong to a union and can get insurance and set up retirement plans through the union. (We'll discuss unions too in more detail in Chapter 2.)

INSURANCE: AN IMPORTANT CONSIDERATION

Insurance isn't the most exciting topic when it comes to thinking about career options, but it's an important one. Plumbers need to consider several types of insurance:

- Health
- Life
- Business

Health and life insurance are concerns for everyone. Health insurance covers you in case you need to see a doctor. And at some point in your life, you will need to see a doctor. Medical debt is no joke. It can—and does—bankrupt people. Medical care is not cheap, and while health insurance can be expensive, you'll be glad you have it when you need to see a doctor or have a hospital stay.

Life insurance is not as much for you as it is for your loved ones. You may be many years from thinking about having a family. However, the reality is that if you have loved ones, you'll want to be sure they're cared for in the event of your death. And life insurance is much easier and less expensive to get when you're young and healthy.

Business insurance for plumbers comes in several types, including liability and tools insurance. However, the most important one is workers' compensation insurance. In some states, you must have workers' compensation insurance to get and maintain your plumbing license. Workers' comp, as it's commonly called, covers medical expenses and lost wages if you or one of your employees is injured on the job. "On the job" is the key phrase here, in case you're wondering how workers' comp differs from health insurance. Health insurance covers you when you have a medical issue for any reason. Workers' comp covers you specifically when that medical issue results from something that happened at work. Sometimes, work injuries can require medical care that isn't usually covered by health insurance. That might include chiropractic care or physical therapy for back injuries, for example. Workers' comp typically covers that.

So you need both health insurance and workers' comp. And given that being plumber is a very physical job that sometimes involves injuries, you'll want to be sure you're covered.

Plumbers can be employed by someone else or self-employed, and each choice has tax and insurance implications.

LET'S TALK ABOUT TAXES

Another important topic is taxes. If you're hired by a company as a regular employee, they'll take taxes out of your paycheck. But as a plumber, you may be self-employed or employed as a contractor. On the surface, that looks like you get a higher paycheck—and indeed you often do. However, that's largely because your employer doesn't have to pay for insurance or taxes for you—you must pay for those yourself. In addition to paying the state and federal taxes that an employer typically takes out, you also must pay a 15.3 percent self-employment tax that goes to cover what an employer would have paid into Medicare and Social Security for you. Essentially, you're covering payments that typically an employer would have covered. That 15.3 percent isn't a small amount, so you'll want to consider that when you think about the type of plumbing job you ultimately want to get.

CHAPTER 2

Getting Started

By now, you'll have read through Chapter 1 and you may have decided that a career as a plumber sounds appealing and a good option. Next, let's look at what you need to do to get there and explore the different areas in the field that might interest you.

DETERMINE WHAT TRAINING YOU NEED

You'll need a high school diploma or GED for all the jobs we'll discuss in this book. You'll want to have a good foundation in math, and it also helps to have a solid base of knowledge in computers. Some of the diagnostic tools that plumbers use involve technology, and if you're designing plumbing for a new build or a repipe, you'll need to use computer-aided design (CAD) tools. A decent background in physics helps too in this job area.

There are two main paths you can take to become a plumber after you finish high school:

- Attend trade school
- Find an apprenticeship

First and foremost, you'll need a high school degree or GED to be a plumber. And then you can decide whether you want to go to trade school or find an apprenticeship.

One benefit to trade school is the chance to meet other people in the field and build connections.

TRADE SCHOOL

Trade schools are for-profit. They offer specialized training in fields like plumbing, and they provide a range of classes. If you select a good trade school, you can be assured that you'll get a solid base of training in the plumbing field that will prepare you well for getting your license and a job in the industry.

There are trade schools all over the country, so you can search in your area to find one that seems like a good fit for your needs. Trade school costs vary widely, so be sure to evaluate the costs of various programs against what you'll learn there. Make sure the trade school you settle on is accredited. This is proof that the school you're attending will prepare you for a job in the field. Typically, trade schools will require that you have a high school diploma or a GED to attend.

CHOOSING AN APPRENTICESHIP

In an apprentice program, you train under an experienced professional in the field. Typically, much of your learning in an apprenticeship will be done in the field—you'll learn on the job. Plumbing apprenticeships usually last for several years, and you are often paid for them. However, the pay is on the lower side since you're still learning.

Plumbing companies may offer apprenticeships. You can also enroll in a community college program that involves an apprenticeship. Typically, these community college programs are offered in partnership with a plumbers' union. They involve a combination of classroom learning and on-the-job apprentice training. Like an apprenticeship through a plumbing company, they take several years to complete. In some cases, you earn an associate's degree or a certificate if you complete a community college apprenticeship program.

BIG OPPORTUNITIES

"There are lots of opportunities in this area. You can travel with the job, work in almost any country, and build a career as you go."

COMMUNITY COLLEGE

If you opt for the community college program, it will likely cost less than a trade school. Many states offer free community college for a set period of time (such as the first year), and community college in general is quite affordable. As with trade school, you'll need a high school diploma or GED to enroll in a community college program. However, many community colleges will allow high school students to take classes while still in high school. So that's an avenue to explore if you're interested in getting a jump on things.

Community college is another way to learn the skills needed to be a good plumber.

WHICH ROUTE TO CHOOSE?

Whether to choose trade school or an apprenticeship is a personal decision, and only you can answer which is best for your particular situation. However, you will pay for trade school, whereas with an

WHAT ARE PIPEFITTERS AND STEAMFITTERS?

We've mentioned unions a couple of times, and will explain them in more detail later in this chapter. But plumbing unions often cover not only plumbers, but also steamfitters and pipefitters—two terms you may or may not be familiar with.

Pipefitters are the people who install, assemble, make, and maintain piping systems. Steamfitters are specialized pipefitters who work on pipe systems for high-pressure materials, such as chemicals, acid, and steam.

HAVE YOU GOT WHAT IT TAKES?

Wondering if you've got what it takes to be a plumber? Here are four more key skills that help contribute to a successful career in the field:

- **Strong communication skills:** You'll need to communicate with customers and/or fellow contractors, so good communication skills are key.
- **Physical fitness:** Plumbing is a physically demanding job. Are you in good shape?
- **Good time-management skills:** When people are having a plumbing problem, they often need it solved quickly and efficiently. Good time-management skills will ensure you're up to the task.
- **Mechanical know-how:** Plumbing can be very complicated, so being mechanically inclined will help you when you're trying to work with complex systems.

apprenticeship you will likely earn some money. But on the other hand, trade schools can often help with job placement when you finish their program, so that may be worth the financial investment.

You can also talk to plumbers in your area and see what they recommend. There may be a terrific trade school near you where you can learn the trade at a reasonable cost—or there may be a local plumbing company that offers great apprenticeships. Talking to people in the field is a great way to narrow down the best option for you.

Physical fitness is a must for plumbers. Climbing under a sink might seem easy now, but as you get older, you'll need to maintain a level of fitness to do this.

Check into the specific licensing requirements for plumbers in your state to make sure you are covered.

GET LICENSED!

Most states require plumbers to be licensed. The requirements for licensing vary by state, so you'll have to check yours. ExploreTheTrades.org is a good place to start; you can click on your state to find links to licensing information, as well as apprenticeships and trade schools. As an example, in California you must have a license to work on any projects in which labor and materials will cost more than $500. You do not, however, need to have a license if you're still learning at the apprentice or journeyman level and you are supervised by a registered contractor. To get your plumbing license in California, you must:

- Be at least 18 years old
- Have a Social Security number or taxpayer identification number (TIN)
- Have a high school diploma or GED
- Have four years of journeyman-level experience or equivalent college/trade school training
- Pay any required fees
- Pass the licensing exam
- Pass a background check
- Prove you have worker's comp insurance (or an exemption, if you qualify)
- Have a contractor's surety bond (a financial guarantee that you'll meet contractual obligations for your customers).

In some cases, licensing is done at a more local level. Kansas, for example, does not offer a state license for plumbers. Instead, licensing is done at the local level. The same is true for Missouri.

As you can see, a lot goes into getting your license. But in most states, you can't work as a plumber without it, so it's a must-do. Check the licensing requirements for the state where you think you'll be working to get an idea of what you'll need to do when you reach the point of entering the workplace.

WORKING YOUR WAY UP

There are several levels you can achieve in your quest to become a plumber. Apprentice plumbers are work at an entry-level position and under a more experienced plumber. They're still learning the trade. It varies by state, but most plumbers are apprentices for around four years before moving up. The next level up is journeyman plumber. They have finished their apprenticeship and passed a licensing exam, and they can work independently. Finally, master plumbers have worked as journeymen for a number of years, typically five. That means they have acquired even more experience, and passed a licensing exam. Master plumbers have a wide breadth of knowledge of the plumbing industry and often supervise newer plumbers. They are often more involved in the design of new plumbing systems and in working with officials from permitting and city code offices.

If you build your skills, make connections in the field, and work hard, you can become a master plumber.

JOINING A UNION

We've mentioned unions a couple of times already, so let's talk a little more about them. You aren't required to join a union. However, in many industries, it's wise to consider it. Plumbers can work in union and non-union shops, and there's no definitive way to say whether one is better than the other. It really depends on the leadership and work environment in any given shop. However, in general, being part of a union means someone has your back, so to speak. If you feel you are being treated poorly by management at your job, for example, you can speak to your union representative. They can advise you or even go to meetings with management on your behalf if needed. In addition, plumbing union members usually earn higher wages than non-union members and have access to insurance and retirement plans.

There are many different unions for plumbers, but one large one is the United Association of Journeymen and Apprentices of the Plumbing and Pipefitting Industry of the United States and Canada, or UA. Approximately 376,000 plumbers, pipefitters, and others in the greater plumbing industry belong to it.

The downside to joining a union? You have to pay dues. These are usually taken directly out of your paycheck, and they typically aren't high. However, they are still a budget consideration.

In a perfect world, your work conditions would be great and you'd never need to strike. But if issues come up in your job, it's good to have a union behind you.

Every St Patrick's Day, the Chicago Journeymen Plumbers Local 130 union dyes the Chicago River green. This fun tradition dates back to 1962.

START LAYING THE GROUND IN HIGH SCHOOL

Now you have a good idea of what's involved on the road to becoming a plumber and the routes to take after you finish school. In the meantime, keep working toward your high school diploma. It really is the key to almost any practical field.

And if you want to get a jump-start on entering the trade, there are some avenues you can explore. As mentioned earlier, many community colleges will allow teens to take classes while still in high school. Some unions offer skilled trade classes to teens, so check with unions local to you to see whether that's an option. You can also investigate volunteer opportunities for teens. You might be surprised how many involve a building component. That especially applies if you're able to travel to an area in need, such as an area that has been devastated by a natural disaster that left many people without their homes.

You can also explore internships and apprenticeships, too. They vary in their age requirements, but some will accept teens younger than 18. The bottom line is opportunities are out there. You just have to look for them and be ready to respond when they come up.

BUSTING MYTHS: NOT JUST FOR MEN

Although plumbing is a heavily male-dominated area, there is plenty of room for women in the field.

Traditionally, the plumbing field has been heavily male-dominated. Sources show that only between 1 and 3 percent of plumbers in the United States are female. Exact numbers are difficult to get because different surveys have different data-collection methods. But, it is still the case that men make up the vast majority of the plumbing industry.

WHERE ARE THE WOMEN?

Plumbing has long been considered “men’s work,” but there’s no good reason for that. The skills that make a good plumber are skills that are not dependent on gender. Some have cited the need to be able to lift heavy items as a reason why more men have historically been in the industry. However, strength is not something only men possess. Strength can be developed through discipline, nutrition, and exercise, all of which are not gender-dependent.

BREAKING DOWN THE BARRIERS

When an industry has long been dominated by individuals from a particular gender, the change to a more balanced workforce representative of the population can be slow. However, some women have been working to bring gender diversity into the plumbing industry.

THEY COULD AND THEY DID!

Hattie Hasan is a plumber and the founder of a leading plumbing company in the United Kingdom (UK). The organization has a register of female tradespeople and 100 of the 750 women on the books are plumbers. Hasan and Leah Robson, also a tradesperson in the UK, are both working to connect more women working in the trades. Hasan worked 17 years in the plumbing industry without meeting another female plumber, so she recognizes how isolating it can be to work in a field dominated by one gender. Hasan and Robson both stress how useful social media has been in connecting female tradespeople around the world.

In the United States, barriers have been broken by Anna Hall. She is the president of P&H Divine Plumbing in Chicago. A lifelong resident of Chicago, Hall broke boundaries by not only being a female plumber, but by being a Black female plumber who has built a very successful business. As Hall states, she "put in her time" to perfect her trade, and then launched a business through which she serves areas that others often don't serve and employs other people from diverse backgrounds. P&H Divine employed 14 plumbers as of 2024, and longer-term plans are to grow by 20 or 30 more. Through hard work and perseverance, Hall has realized her dream of building a great business that is staffed by skilled plumbers from diverse backgrounds.

The plumbing industry is now beginning to see more diversity within its workforce.

CHAPTER 3

Different Jobs and Different Environments

In this chapter, we'll discuss the different work environments you can expect to choose from as a plumber. The work environment is the physical space, working conditions, and general approach that is part of a job. Work environment greatly impacts how we feel at work and whether we enjoy our work. For that reason, it's an important consideration as you think about your future career. As a plumber, you'll have several different options for work environment, so you're sure to find one that suits you.

RESIDENTIAL PLUMBING

Residential plumbers work in people's houses. They typically work on many aspects of residential plumbing. That includes water heaters, fixtures (such as sink and shower fixtures), and water, drain, and sewer lines. If a person has a plumbing issue in their home, they call a residential plumber—and most often, the residential plumber can handle it. Occasionally, a problem might require more contractors as well, for example, if a burst pipe has caused major damage to the house. However, in general plumbers can fix the plumbing issues and the minor patchwork that may go with it.

As a residential plumber, you'd need to be familiar with all building codes and ensure that a home's plumbing meets the regulations for residential plumbing. It is particularly the case that in older homes, plumbing may need to be replaced. That is a

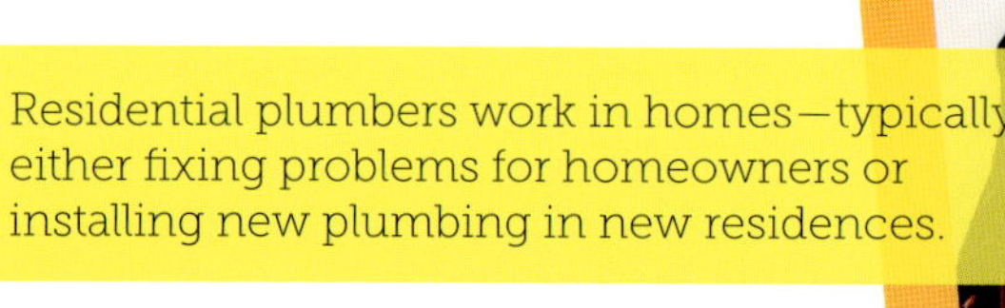

Residential plumbers work in homes—typically either fixing problems for homeowners or installing new plumbing in new residences.

major job—and a major expense for the homeowner. When a residential plumber repipes a house, it is their job to make sure the work meets all building codes.

In this role you'll work in people's homes. For this particular plumbing job, excellent people skills are a real benefit because the people you are working for will want to feel comfortable having you in their home. So you'll need to be personable and professional when you arrive, throughout the job, and as you're completing your work.

In commercial plumbing, you'd work with construction forepeople or building managers, rather than homeowners.

COMMERCIAL PLUMBING

As a commercial plumber you would work mainly on commercial business buildings, such as stores, but you might also work on large housing developments, such as apartment complexes. Whereas a residential plumber may need to fix a toilet and the house's associated sewer line, a commercial plumber may need to fix an extensive waste removal system for an entire apartment block. You'd also have more familiarity with complex plumbing systems than most residential plumbers do.

Some commercial plumbers work on new commercial construction. In this instance, you'd install plumbing systems designed to support the needs of many people at any given time. To do so, you'd need to be able to read construction blueprints and understand how to install complex plumbing systems. You might also work on boiler systems, which typically aren't found in newer residential homes. (Boilers used to be common in homes, but now forced-air furnaces are much more common in American homes. Like residential plumbers, commercial plumbers must know the codes and regulations for their region and make sure the projects they work on meet those standards.

WORKING WITH OTHER PEOPLE

As a commercial plumber, you won't work with homeowners. Rather, you'll work with building managers and facilities or maintenance managers. You may also work with other construction people working on other aspects of the commercial property. So you'll still need people skills, to some extent, but going into a commercial building is very different from entering someone's personal home. After the building manager or whoever is in charge lets you in and shows you the problem, they'll likely leave you alone to do your work. They will just check in with you every now and then. Some homeowners will do the same, but some are more eager to see exactly what you're doing to their home.

THE ROLE OF INDUSTRIAL PLUMBER

Industrial plumbing is somewhat like commercial plumbing in that you'd work on large buildings, rather than smaller homes. However, commercial plumbers tend to work on commercial and retail buildings, schools, and other similar sizeable buildings. Industrial plumbers tend to work on factories, power plants, production plants, and similar spaces. There is some crossover between commercial and industrial plumbers, and sometimes the terms are used interchangeably. But there can be a difference, since industrial plumbers may need to work on systems that involve factors such as eyewash stations and hazardous waste disposal.

Much like commercial plumbers, industrial plumbers work in buildings rather than in individual homes.

FIVE KEYS TO A HEALTHY WORK ENVIRONMENT

To some extent, it's difficult to know whether a work environment is a good one until you've worked in it. However, there are some signs of a healthy work environment that you can look for when you're considering any job. These environments typically have:

- **Trust:** Managers trust employees to do their jobs, and employees trust managers to have their back and to support them as needed.
- **Cooperation:** Employees and managers work together and collaborate well on projects. Their focus is working as a tightly knit team to get the best results.
- **Listening:** Employees and managers listen to each other's concerns with an open mind and consideration.
- **Communication:** Managers communicate effectively with their teams, and teams communicate well within themselves, too.
- **Clarity:** Expectations are clear to everyone. There is no confusion.

As an industrial plumber you would need to have a good knowledge of building codes and regulations. You'd also need to understand environmental regulations and keep up to date with them. That is because you may have to deal with hazardous materials, depending on the project you are working on. Industrial plumbers also work on features such as storm drains.

As with residential and commercial plumbers, industrial plumbers typically spend a lot of time working inside. However, they don't go into people's homes. Rather, they go into large buildings and may work with facilities managers, other construction personnel, and people from the local building offices.

QUALIFICATIONS AND TRAINING

For all of the jobs described in this chapter, you'll need a high school diploma or GED. You'll also need a valid driver's license and a clean background check, since you'll be driving to different jobs. You'll also need either a trade school background or an apprenticeship.

WHAT'S THE PAY?

The average median pay for plumbers across the United States was $61,550 as of 2024, according to the BLS. Pay varies greatly, though, depending on where you work and what type of business you work for. It also depends on whether you're an apprentice, journeyman, or master plumber.

RESIDENTIAL OR COMMERCIAL/INDUSTRIAL

If you're weighing which type of work environment you might prefer, it might help to explore some of the differences between residential and commercial/industrial plumbing:

- **Usage:** Residential plumbing gets a lot less use than commercial plumbing, meaning there's less wear and tear on residential plumbing in most cases.
- **Maintenance:** Commercial and industrial plumbers do a lot more maintenance work to try to keep systems working well and to prevent problems from occurring. Residential plumbers rarely do maintenance work—they are called when a problem occurs.
- **Complexity:** Commercial and industrial plumbing systems are typically much more complex, and the buildings are generally larger (sometimes much larger). A US home generally has somewhere between two and four toilets—sometimes more, sometimes fewer. A commercial building could have upward of 20. And that's not to mention sinks, water fountains, water heaters, and boilers.
- **Damage potential:** Usually, a residential plumbing issue doesn't cause too much damage. Of course, there are cases where, for example, a washing machine on the second floor has a burst water line. In that instance, there may be damage to the floor below the washer—which could be the living room ceiling! But in general, most homeowners catch plumbing issues before they cause too much damage. However, because commercial and industrial systems are much larger and more complex, there is much greater chance of a great deal of damage occurring. Another factor is that commercial and industrial systems are used by more people, which increases the chance of damage.
- **Water heaters:** Not surprisingly, commercial water heaters are much larger and more complex than residential water heaters.
- **Drainage:** Like everything else, drainage is more complex in commercial and industrial plumbing. It may take several tries to figure out which sewer line is causing a backup down the line. However, in residential

Both residential plumbing and commercial plumbing have a lot to offer people who are interested in entering the plumbing trade.

plumbing, determining where a problem is coming from is generally straightforward and easy to trace.

- **Tools:** Residential plumbers use tools, of course—pipe wrenches, snakes, plungers, and the like. But commercial and industrial plumbers have a more specialized set of tools for large-scale, complex projects. These can include industrial wet/dry vacuums, tile saws, and large drain cleaners.
- **Work hours:** Some residential plumbers work any time of day or night—they specialize in emergency repairs, which means they have to respond to emergency call-outs at any hour. But many work a more standard eight-hour workday, with weekends off. Commercial plumbers often need to work odd hours or weekends because their work is best done when the building is free of customers or employees.

CHAPTER 4

Specializing in the Plumbing Industry

In the previous chapter, we discussed the three big types of work environments for plumbers. However, there are other, more specialized areas of the plumbing industry you can explore, too. In this chapter, we'll look at some more specialized jobs within the plumbing industry.

THE ROLE OF A PIPEFITTER

Often when you read about plumbing, you read about pipefitters. But pipefitters don't just work on residential pipes, for example. They work on a wide variety of types of pipes. Pipefitters install, maintain, and repair piping systems. They thread and weld together piping systems. These systems may be for liquid transport (such as water or waste), but they may also be for oil, chemicals, gas, and more. Depending on the project, pipefitters may lay and fit pipes outdoors or indoors. For example, every street with water infrastructure has a water main in it. Pipefitters may have helped the pipelayer to install these water mains in the street when the street was being developed. Or they may

Large infrastructure projects often require much larger pipes than residential projects.

Steamfitters do similar work to pipefitters, but on very specific types of pipes that carry high-pressure materials.

have piped a building that is fed by the water main, in which case they would have worked indoors. So, as a pipefitter, depending on the project, you may work inside or outside. That can be a good or a bad thing, depending on how you feel about working in weather conditions that may or may not be favorable!

QUALIFICATIONS AND TRAINING

To be a pipefitter, you'll need a high school diploma or GED. You'll also need a valid driver's license and a clean background check, since you'll be driving to different jobs. Also required is a trade school background or an apprenticeship.

WHAT'S THE PAY?

The pay for pipefitters is roughly the same as that for plumbers, though in some areas pipefitters make a bit more than plumbers. But overall, the difference in salary is not great, and likely won't be a deciding factor in choosing between pipefitting or plumbing as your career of choice.

WORKING AS A STEAMFITTER

A steamfitter, as mentioned earlier, is a specific type of pipefitter. Steamfitters work on piping systems that are used for high-pressure materials, such as steam, acid, or other hazardous chemicals. As a steamfitter, you'd typically work in industrial plumbing environments, such as factories. In addition to welding and fitting pipes as a pipefitter does, you would also have to test pressurization using special gauges and other specific measurement tools.

QUALIFICATIONS AND TRAINING

To be a steamfitter, you'll need a high school diploma or GED. You'll also need a valid driver's license and a clean background check, because you will need to travel for your work. You'll also need either a trade school background or an apprenticeship.

If outdoor work and construction vehicles appeal to you, you might want to consider becoming a pipelayer.

NO DESK NEEDED!

"I never wanted to sit behind a desk, and with this job, you don't have to. You spend most of your time on your feet and moving around. It's an active job."

WHAT'S THE PAY?

Steamfitters and pipefitters make similar salaries. However, there is one important consideration if you're thinking about steamfitting, and that is safety. Steamfitters may work with hazardous materials and be exposed to chemicals or contaminants. As such, most steamfitters must wear protective gear and practice hazardous materials safety to do their job.

OUTDOOR WORK: PIPELAYER

While pipefitters may sometimes help with outdoor work, typically the bulk of that work is performed by pipelayers. Pipelayers generally work in the construction industry and help lay the plumbing infrastructure necessary when new construction, such as a housing development or a retail complex, is being built. In this role, you would lay pipes in underground trenches. You might also be responsible for piping water, gas, and sewage systems. If driving large construction equipment such as backhoes and excavators appeals to you, you might consider a job in pipelaying, since you'll have to use those machines to trench out the areas where the pipes will be laid.

While pipefitters may work outside from time to time but mostly work inside, pipelayers work almost exclusively outside. So you have to be ready, and willing, to work in all types of weather conditions!

Pipelayers also must have a good understanding of slope and grading to position pipes appropriately. It needs to be done right the first time, or it won't pass inspection.

QUALIFICATIONS AND TRAINING

To be a pipelayer, you'll need a high school diploma or GED, a valid driver's license, and a clean background check. Like the other jobs discussed so far, you'll be traveling a lot for work. You'll also need either a trade school background or an apprenticeship.

WHAT'S THE PAY?

Pipelayers typically make a bit less than plumbers, pipefitters, and steamfitters. It all depends on the job and the area, of course, but in general, the salary is a little lower for pipelayers. Still, if you enjoy working outside and want to be part of the basic infrastructure for construction projects, this is an area of the plumbing field that might appeal to you.

A WORLD OF OPPORTUNITY

As you can see, there are several outside-the-box opportunities for people interested in a career in plumbing but not necessarily interested in making house calls or working late nights. There are far too many options to discuss in one chapter, but hopefully we've covered a few to give you some food for thought as you consider your future career in the plumbing field. Your career options really are wide open in the plumbing industry, which gives you a lot of room to find the niche that perfectly fits your skills, interests, and career aims.

One consideration about becoming a pipelayer is pay. It tends to be on the lower end of the payscale for plumbing careers.

A DAY IN THE LIFE: PIPEFITTER

Being a pipefitter might not seem like the most glamorous of jobs in the plumbing industry, but there's more to it than you might think.

On any given day, pipefitters use saws, pipe threaders, pipe benders, and cutting torches to cut, thread, and hammer pipes to specifications following the directions in the blueprints. They mark the pipes for cutting and threading them.

Pipefitters then use those same blueprints to lay out full-scale drawings of pipe systems, which are used for layout, installation, and repair. They then physically assemble the pipes, tubes, and fittings. This is done by threading joints, welding, soldering, and sometimes brazing and cementing. (Brazing is similar to welding and soldering, but at a different temperature.)

Some parts of the job aren't done every day, but are done regularly. For example, pipefitters regularly use pressure gauges, hydrostatic testing, and other test methods to inspect and examine installed pipe systems.

Pipefitting is a very physical, hands-on job—and typically one where you're not working directly with customers.

If variety appeals to you, pipefitting might be a good choice. Because many tasks fall to the pipefitter, there's a lot of variety in their work day.

At times, they install automatic controls to help regulate the pipe system. When needed, they remove and replace faulty or worn parts of the system. Some pipefitters even get to install pipe systems that support alternative energy systems, such as geothermal heating and cooling systems. This last task is becoming more common as the United States focuses on energy-saving solutions to help protect the environment.

FULL OF VARIETY

"I really like the challenge of being a pipefitter. I never wanted to do a job that would be the same every day. In this job, no two days are alike. One day I might be working on a layout of pipe systems, the next day I may be called in to test a faulty system. It keeps me alert, and I'm always learning something new as the industry changes."

CHAPTER 5

Alternative Routes into Plumbing

We've talked about the standard ways to break into the plumbing industry and the typical work environments you might find. But there are always other approaches and avenues to a given goal. In this chapter, we'll talk about some of the other niche areas you might want to explore.

THE MILITARY AND PLUMBING

The military might not be on your radar if you're thinking about a career in plumbing. However, it is an option if you're not interested in trade school. The military provides training for many careers, and plumbing is one of them. Enlisting in the military doesn't necessarily mean you're going to fight on the front lines. Often, it means you're doing the same types of jobs as nonmilitary workers, just for the military. And the bonus is that you get paid for your service and training. (You typically get paid for civilian apprenticeships through a community college or a union, too. But obviously you don't get paid if you're attending trade school —rather, you're paying them.)

If you need to be paid to learn plumbing skills, the military might be a good option.

The great thing about military training is that you take the skills with you when you are discharged.

WHAT YOU'LL LEARN

In the army, for example, a plumber typically performs the same general duties as a plumber who works outside of the military. You'll learn plumbing, pipefitting, maintenance, and repairs. Construction and planning are also included. So when you leave the military (at whatever point you choose to do so), you will leave with a wide breadth of experience in the plumbing field.

TRAINING PROVIDED

When you enlist in the army, you'll go through ten weeks of basic training. That provides you with rigorous physical training, weapons training, military life and customs training, and tactical and survival skills training. You'll then get seven weeks of advanced individual training. And there are 52 nationally recognized certifications available.

BENEFITS AND REWARDS

The army offers pay above the federal minimum wage. It also provides health insurance, allowances for food, clothing, and housing, and education benefits. And if you decide to become a career military person (staying enlisted for longer than the minimum enlistment period), the retirement benefits can be quite significant. Some people who serve in the military choose to serve for 20 years so they can retire with a high pension. They retire from the military in their late thirties and then take a civilian job. They then earn regular pay plus a significant military pension. Essentially, they receive double pay for the remainder of their working days.

You're eligible to work as a plumber for the army if you're in the army, the army reserve, or the army national guard. It's an entry-level position.

WHAT YOU NEED

If you want to pursue your plumbing training in the army, you'll need to be at least 17 years old and a US citizen or permanent resident with a valid Green Card. You'll also need a high school diploma or GED—as is the case for virtually all jobs in the plumbing world.

You'll have to have a clean criminal record (the army refers to it as "no major law violations") and no major medical concerns. You'll also have to meet their tattoo guidelines.

OTHER AREAS OF THE MILITARY

The army isn't the only branch of the military to use professionals in the greater plumbing field. The marines uses water support technicians, who do a lot of plumbing-type work on water supplies and water purification systems. The air force uses water and fuel systems maintenance personnel. And the navy has several different job descriptions within the field of plumbing. So depending on what you want to do and which branch of the military interests you most, there are opportunities in the plumbing field within the military.

If you decide to consider the military as your entry into the plumbing field, you can talk to a military recruiter and take the Armed Services Vocational Aptitude Battery (ASVAB) to see whether your skills line up with what the military is looking for in a plumber.

ENLISTING IS A SERIOUS BUSINESS

Starting your plumbing career by getting your training in the military might sound very appealing. What's not to like? You get paid, there are a lot of extra benefits offered, and you get quality training to set you up in your career. However, joining the military is a huge commitment and not to be taken lightly. When you enlist in the military (and you must enlist to be eligible for their training), you are committing to serve your country. It is against the law to "quit." So once you're in, you're in—unless you have a very compelling reason to leave. In that case you might be granted an honorable discharge.

The other important point about being in the military is that when you commit to serve your country, you commit to go where they need you to go and do what they need you to do. If the United States were to go to war while you were enlisted, you could very well find yourself on the front lines. And even during peace time, military life typically comes with many moves. So if you're the type of person who likes to settle in one place and not move around a lot, the military life will likely not appeal to you.

If you're considering joining the military to train in plumbing, be sure you're ready for the rigors of military life and the expectations that come with it.

HEAD FOR THE TOP: PLUMBING INSPECTOR

Maybe you're interested in plumbing but you're not sure you want to spend your career doing work such as repairing clogged drains, pipelaying, or steamfitting. If that is the case, another career area that you might consider is working as a plumbing inspector.

We've mentioned that plumbers need to know building codes and regulations so they can ensure their work complies. Where's the check and balance on this system? It's the city (or county) plumbing inspector. Any time a new property is built or substantial renovations are done, the construction company must file for permits and have the local authority come out and inspect the work that is done. If the work hasn't been done correctly (or "to code"), the permit will not be issued. And if the permit isn't issued, construction must be halted, and the problems have to be corrected as needed.

As a plumbing inspector, you'd be the person who would look over a jobsite and determine whether the work has been done correctly. To do this job, you generally need to be at least a journeyman plumber, though often it's required that you be a master plumber. You need to be able to read blueprints (which have already gone through an approval process). You then must determine whether the plumbing work follows the blueprints and meets the building codes and

Eventually, a skilled plumber can work their way up to a career as a plumbing inspector, which commands a good salary.

regulations. When it doesn't, you issue citations and recommend corrective measures that can be taken to resolve the problems.

Generally, the plumbing inspector then follows up and goes back out to reinspect the jobsite. They check if the corrections have been made and the plumbing is up to code. In some cases, plumbing inspectors may even be called upon to testify in court if there is a legal issue that has arisen from a problem with plumbing.

QUALIFICATIONS AND TRAINING

To be a plumbing inspector, you'll need a high school diploma or GED. You'll also need a clean background check and a valid driving license, so you can drive to jobsites. You'll also need either a trade school background or an apprenticeship. You'll need a solid knowledge of your area's building codes and related legislation. You'll also need to know the various specifications for different types of plumbing systems.

Some areas will require you to be a licensed journeyman or master plumber to become a plumbing inspector. Most require you to have at least four to seven years of experience. You may also need to have a separate inspector's license. You can research the requirements in your area if this is a career path that you think might interest you.

MOVING ON TO BIGGER AND BETTER THINGS

When thinking about your career, you want to consider both the short and the long term. Where do you want to start and where do you want to be in 10, 20, or 30 years? Only you can answer that. But in general, in trades such as plumbing, you need to be willing to start at the bottom and move up. Even if you invest in trade school, you still need to start as an apprentice, work your way to journeyman plumber, and eventually to master plumber. And the plus side is that as you're working your way up from the bottom, you have the opportunity to learn a lot–a lot of skills, but also a lot about what you like.

WHAT'S THE PAY?

The salary for a plumbing inspector is highly dependent on area—for example, plumbing inspectors in high-priced cities make significantly more than plumbing inspectors in smaller, less expensive cities. But across the board, plumbing inspectors typically make a strong salary that aligns with what a master plumber makes.

CERTIFICATIONS, CERTIFICATIONS, AND MORE CERTIFICATIONS!

In virtually all the trades, there are certifications you can earn that will help improve your earning power and your skill set. And the plumbing career is no different. Some of the certifications available include:

- **Backflow prevention certification:** Backflow preventers ensure that contaminated water doesn't reenter main water supplies. This certification is for plumbers who want to work in installing and maintaining these systems.
- **Medical gas installer certification:** In hospital and nursing home settings, medical gasses must be delivered safely to patients. (Certain gasses are flammable, so safety is a must.) The certification to install and maintain medical gas systems requires a high level of training, and you must be a journeyman or master plumber to earn it.
- **Rainwater catchment system certification:** Rainwater catchment systems are becoming increasingly common as people recognize the need for water conservation in our changing environment, as we become more aware of increasing temperatures and the threat of drought. This certification is for plumbers who want to install, design, and inspect these systems.
- **Water-based fire protection systems certification:** This certification is for people who want to inspect, test, and maintain fire protection systems. These are mandatory in all homes and buildings in the United States.
- **Infection control and water quality certification:** Proper plumbing and piping is required to prevent the spread of certain infectious diseases from waterborne and other pathogens. (Cholera, for example, is one disease that is spread when people don't have access to clean water supplies.) This certification allows plumbers to safeguard public health and prevent the spread of disease.
- **Hydronic heating and cooling certification:** Hydronic heating and cooling uses water to heat and cool spaces. It is considered an energy-efficient heating and cooling method, and this certification prepares plumbers who want to install and maintain such systems.

Plumbing is a trade with many certifications, which can only help boost your career and earning potential, so earning them is beneficial.

YOU EARN RESPECT

"I've never been to a job where someone hasn't been thankful. People respect what you do and if you do it fast and well, they are really grateful. That feels good."

This is just a sampling of the many available certifications for plumbers. They are listed by the American Society of Sanitary Engineering (ASSE) International, which has been serving the plumbing industry for more than 100 years. As more and more energy-efficient solutions become available, no doubt more certifications will arise. For example, Leadership in Energy and Environmental Design (LEED) certification is available for plumbers and is becoming a more common certification to pursue. LEED certification is great for plumbers who are environmentally conscious and want to ensure they are embracing sustainable solutions in plumbing as they carry out their work.

Certifications will set you apart in the field and can help improve your earning power, so keep an eye out for ones that appeal to you as you embark on your plumbing career.

CHAPTER 6

Your Career Future

When you're considering a career, it's crucial to look at the future and how that career may look. While it is impossible to know exactly what will happen many years from now, you can look at the information available today and what that suggests about the future of the industry.

THE FUTURE FOR PLUMBERS

The future holds some exciting changes for plumbers. In general, the BLS expects job growth for plumbers, pipefitters, and steamfitters to grow at a rate of about 2 percent over the next decade. That is in step with general job growth projects across occupations. Sprinkler fitters in particular are expected to have more job growth. That is because building codes are continuing to change to require more advanced fire-prevention systems in buildings.

NEW TRENDS IN PLUMBING

In addition to job growth, a continuing focus on the environment is leading to some exciting advancements in the plumbing sector.

Water conservation is becoming a focus in more and more parts of the United States. It has long been a major concern in drought-prone states such as California. However, even some states that used to get plenty of rain, such as those in the Pacific Northwest, are now regularly facing threat from drought, too. As such, there is great demand for water conservation solutions —and qualified professionals to install and maintain them.

SWITCHING TO TANKLESS

Water heaters used to have large tanks, many holding up to 50 gallons of water. The heating technology for such water heaters is wildly inefficient, heating a great deal of water that isn't being used. Tankless water heaters are becoming more and more common.

Water conservation is an issue in many places in the United States. Smart plumbers will become familiar with water-conservation technologies and how to install and maintain them.

That is because the Department of Energy (DoE) highlights the energy savings from tankless water heaters at about 25 percent. As more and more households switch to tankless water heaters, qualified technicians and plumbers will be needed to install them.

GRAYWATER SYSTEMS

Graywater is wastewater that comes from showers, baths, washing machines, and sinks. (Blackwater, in contrast, is wastewater that comes from toilets and can contain human waste.) Because graywater doesn't contain human waste, it is relatively "clean" and can be reused for things like watering the yard. It should not be ingested by humans or pets, but it's fine for nonpotable uses. Graywater systems are designed to collect and recycle graywater. So as more homeowners become water-conscious, there will be a greater demand for plumbing professionals to install and maintain the systems.

SMART AND INFRARED

Infrared and smart pipe technology are both used to detect leaks and/or excess moisture. These relatively new technologies can make plumbers' jobs easier and more efficient. Plumbers trained in this new technology will be able to solve problems more quickly. That means they will be able to see many more customers, thanks to the time-saving technology.

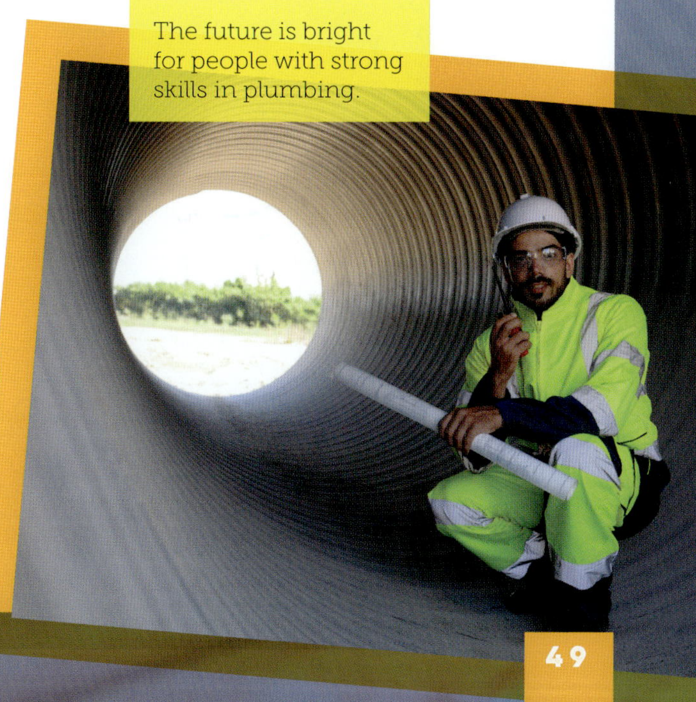

The future is bright for people with strong skills in plumbing.

SMART PLUMBING FIXTURES

In addition to smart pipes, there are smart plumbing systems and fixtures designed to reduce water usage, increase sanitation, and generally make people's lives a lot more efficient. They are also sometimes fun, such as in the case of Bluetooth-enabled showerheads that can stream your favorite music while you take a shower.

Touchless faucets allow users to turn on the water without touching the fixture. That is important for sanitation when hands may be contaminated with bacteria from uncooked food in the kitchen or other germs in other areas of the house. For example, certain colds and flus spread very easily but spread can be reduced by handwashing. But if the person with the illness touches the bathroom faucet to wash their hands and then doesn't wipe it down with a cleaner, the next person to use that faucet can pick up the germs. Touchless faucets also help reduce water usage. That is because most of them shut off after a short time, in case the person has walked away from the faucet without turning it off. Smart toilets, too, are gaining popularity. Some can even clean and disinfect themselves.

Smart tools and new technologies are unlikely to cost plumbers their jobs. Instead, they'll allow them to work more efficiently, which can translate to more overall pay.

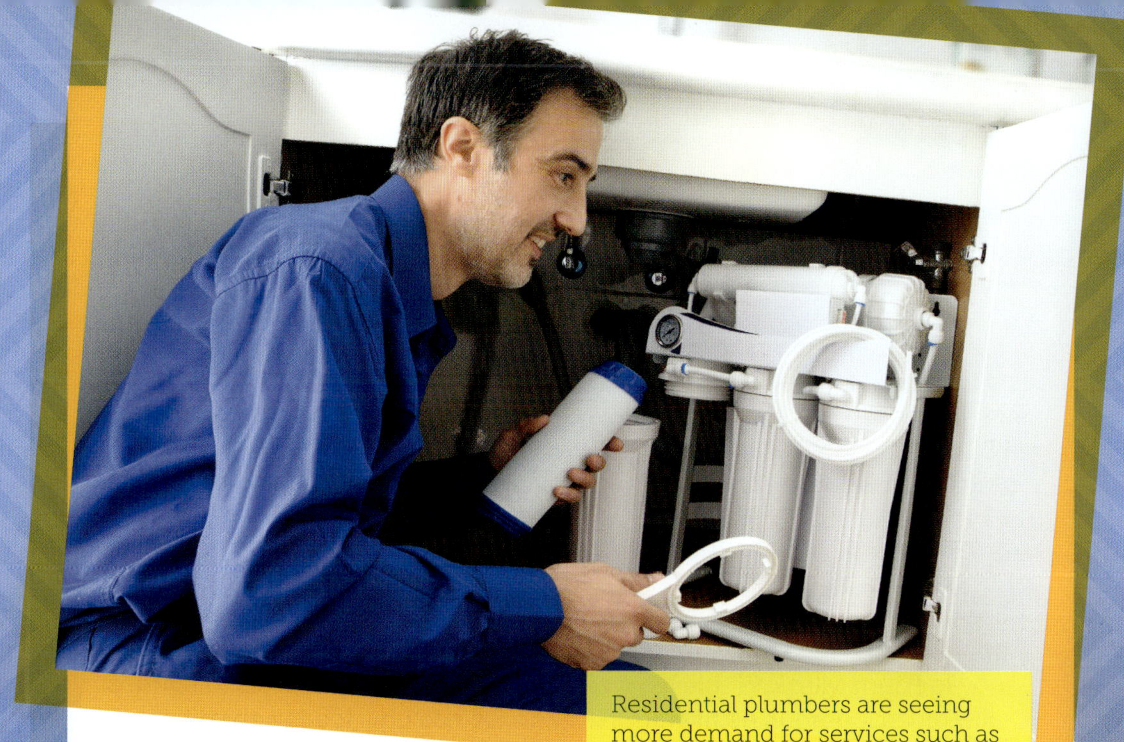

Residential plumbers are seeing more demand for services such as installing water filtration systems and water-saving technologies.

As people remodel their homes and as new homes are built, smart fixtures will likely be in high demand—as will the professionals who are trained to install them.

WATER FILTRATION SYSTEMS

Reverse osmosis systems act like water purification systems. They remove contaminants from water using a system that forces water through a semipermeable membrane. Another type of water filtration system gaining popularity is UV water purification. Ultraviolet (UV) light waves are used to kill harmful bacteria in the water. Water filtration systems like these are becoming increasingly common in homes and businesses, and qualified professionals are needed to install the systems and then maintain them too.

ACCESSIBLE PLUMBING

The US population is aging—the Baby Boomer generation born at the end of World War II (1939–1945) are generally in their eighties, and many are even older. With people living longer lives now, it's likely we will continue to have a significant older population. As such, there is a need for accessible plumbing fixtures. Older and disabled individuals often need taller toilets and lower sinks. They may require showers with removable showerheads and may also need accessible showers or bathtubs. Qualified plumbing professionals who can install these items are in demand and will likely continue to be as the population ages.

NEEDING BACKUPS

Particularly in areas where homes have basements, more and more homeowners are installing backup water systems. Essentially, these systems use their home's water supply to power a sump pump that can prevent basement flooding. Sump pumps activate when the ground around your home becomes saturated by heavy rain. The pumps then divert the water that would otherwise collect in the basement into a storm drain. But traditionally, sump pumps have required power. When heavy rainfall occurs, it's not all that unusual for the power to go out. Then homeowners end up with a very wet or flooded basement. New water-powered sump pumps reduce the risk of basement flooding and so are gaining popularity with homeowners. Qualified plumbing professionals are needed to install these systems.

FUTURE-FORWARD: CALIFORNIA

As mentioned, water conservation is becoming an issue in many states. California is the third-largest state in area and by far the most populated state with more than 39 million people as of the 2020 US Census. California has adopted many forward-thinking policies and has long prioritized eco-conscious practices. California is no stranger to water shortages and much of the state is perpetually considered to be in a drought. The state lacks water but has a lot of people who need it.

With its water issues, it is no surprise that California is often at the head of new ideas in water conservation and new regulations to encourage residents to conserve water. Such regulations include things like requirements for low-flow showerheads and kitchen faucets and low-flush toilets. They also include requirements that landscaping can only be watered with sprinklers on certain days of the week and for certain times. Where possible, water-saving drip irrigation systems should be used in place of sprinklers. Common areas must be watered with nonpotable water, to conserve potable water for drinking and cooking.

There are obvious environmental plusses to these practices. The other upside is that there's a big market for plumbing professionals to install, repair, and maintain the systems that help the state be as water-conscious as possible. Plumbing professionals with "green" certifications are in high demand in this future-thinking state.

MOVING FORWARD

So, there you have it: The plumbing industry has a lot to offer, and you have a lot to offer it. If you think this might be the career path you want to pursue, look into ways you can jump-start your learning. Community colleges often allow high school students to take classes, and the local plumbing union in your area may offer training as well. And of course, there's always YouTube. Many different tutorials are available on there, and you can learn a lot about DIY plumbing from there. The future is bright in plumbing —make the most of it!

Whether you decide to work in residential, commercial, or industrial plumbing and whether you choose to be self-employed or work for someone else, there are exciting opportunities in the plumbing industry.

IT KEEPS YOUR BRAIN ACTIVE

"Not only does the job keep you physically fit, it keeps you mentally fit too. You'll have to figure out what the problem is and how to solve it. That keeps you sharp."

MORE PRACTICAL CAREERS

There are many exciting jobs that you could enjoy in the plumbing industry. We've picked out some of them. There are many others to choose from too. If none of the jobs on the following pages fit your dream career, just turn to pages 62–63. There you'll find links to sites at which you can research even more plumbing jobs.

SPRINKLER FITTER

Sprinkler fitters aren't people who install lawn sprinklers—that is typically done by landscapers. Instead, sprinkler fitters are plumbing professionals who install, test, inspect, maintain, and certify fire sprinklers in all types of buildings and structures. Building codes require all commercial structures to have fire sprinklers. Residences in some areas must also have fire sprinklers, but that depends on the state and local area where the residence is located.

QUALIFICATIONS AND TRAINING

People interested in becoming sprinkler fitters must have a high school diploma or GED. They must also have completed an apprenticeship and passed a certification exam. They should have a strong knowledge of plumbing codes and fire protection standards too. More specific requirements vary by place and position, with some sprinkler fitter jobs requiring applicants to have a certification as well. Because sprinkler fitters travel to jobsites, a clean driving record and a valid driver's license is required.

Checking plumbing systems within buildings for safety is an important task.

Plumbers are needed for gas and oil pipelines, too. That is another career area to explore.

GREAT IF YOU LIKE PLANNING

"I like the planning aspect of the job. As a gas pipeline surveyor, you need to be able to look ahead and consider a lot of different factors then figure out a workable plan."

GAS PLUMBER

If dealing with water isn't your thing, you might want to consider a career as a gas plumber. Gas plumbers install, repair, and maintain gas piping systems. Leak detection and repair is a big part of being a gas plumber, since gas is often flammable and can be deadly (depending on the type of gas).

QUALIFICATIONS AND TRAINING

People interested in a career as a gas plumber must have a high school diploma or GED. They must have completed an apprenticeship and passed a certification exam. They also need a knowledge of building codes and gas-safety standards. More specific requirements vary by position, with some requiring additional certifications.

GAS PIPELINE SURVEYOR

Gas pipeline surveyors look at the big picture. They survey the landscape at a possible site for gas extraction to determine whether it's a viable location. They typically use GPS (global positioning system) and GIS (geographic information system) tools to help determine site viability.

QUALIFICATIONS AND TRAINING

Those interested in a career as a gas pipeline surveyor need a high school diploma or GED. Experience in the gas, oil, or construction industries is preferred. Any education or certification in surveying tools, such as GIS, is also preferred. Also, an ability to travel to rural areas is a must since most gas pipeline sites are off the beaten path. A driver's license and clean driving record are also typically required.

PIPELINE INSPECTOR

Pipeline inspectors conduct regular inspections on pipelines to ensure there are no leaks or safety issues and to make sure pipelines comply with all local, state, and federal regulations. The inspectors not only inspect the pipes, they also recommend repairs where needed. Typically, they work in the construction, oil, or gas industry.

QUALIFICATIONS AND TRAINING

Pipeline inspectors need to have a high school diploma or GED. They must also have a strong knowledge of area building codes and safety requirements. They also need to be aware of local, state, and federal regulations. They must also have a certification related to the field—a Construction Inspector certification is a common one. Because pipeline inspectors travel to jobsites, a clean driving record and a valid driver's license are typically required.

WATER HEATER TECHNICIAN

Water heater technicians install, repair, and maintain water heaters. They may do this in residential or in commercial or industrial properties. Some water heater technicians specialize in newer technologies, such as tankless water heaters.

QUALIFICATIONS AND TRAINING

People interested in a career as a water heater technician must have a high school diploma or GED. They also must have knowledge of both plumbing and electrical systems, since many water heaters run on electrical power. In most states, water heater technicians must have a valid plumbing contractor's license. There are sometimes additional licensing requirements for people who want to work on large commercial water heaters and boilers. A clean driving record and a valid driver's license is typically required.

LANDSCAPE IRRIGATION TECHNICIAN

Landscape irrigation technicians install, repair, and maintain systems that deliver water to landscaping and crops. In areas where cold winters are the norm, they often also help winterize such systems.

QUALIFICATIONS AND TRAINING

People interested in a career as a landscape irrigation technician need a high school diploma or GED, which are required for most jobs, and secondary education through a community college or trade school is a plus. Depending on the job, backflow certification may be required. And because many landscape irrigation technicians travel between jobsites, a clean driving record is required.

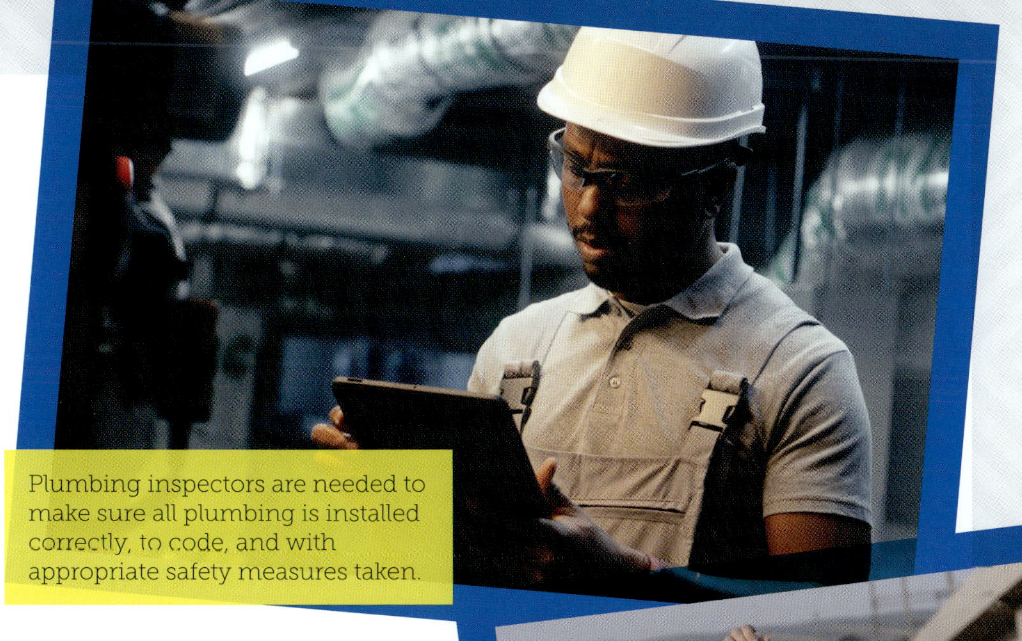

Plumbing inspectors are needed to make sure all plumbing is installed correctly, to code, and with appropriate safety measures taken.

WASTEWATER TREATMENT OPERATOR

This job may not sound all that glamorous, but it's quite important. Wastewater treatment operators work in water treatment plants to help make safe and potable water. They help maintain the treatment system parts, test water samples, and troubleshoot problems. If you enjoy clean drinking water, thank a wastewater treatment operator!

Wastewater treatment operators are the people who keep our drinking water safe—among many other tasks they perform.

QUALIFICATIONS AND TRAINING

Wastewater treatment operators must have a high school diploma or GED. Some secondary education (an associate or bachelor's degree) is preferred for most positions, but it's not always required. What is required, typically, is certification in the field, so you'll need to be prepared to take certification classes and pass an exam.

IMPORTANT WORK

"Providing people with clean drinking water is one of the most important things you can do—it's a crucial job."

WHAT'S NEXT? YOUR CAREER CHECKLIST

As you can see, there are almost endless career opportunities for plumbers, and the future of the industry only looks set to be even more dynamic. So what steps do you need to take to launch your plumbing future? Let's take a look at some questions you need to ask and steps you need to take.

QUESTIONS TO ASK ABOUT SCHOOLS AND COURSES

- Is the program accredited? (Whether you choose trade school or an apprenticeship through a community college, this is an important question. Accredited programs guarantee that you'll get a quality education. They also look far better to potential employers than unaccredited programs.)
- What types of training and classes are offered in your program?
- Do you offer specialty programs in different areas of the field?
- How rigorous is the program? (You need to know how much time to devote to your studies daily. Some people attend community college part time while they work, but some programs may require that you devote yourself to them full time.)
- How much hands-on training does your program allow, compared to classroom learning?
- What certifications can I earn upon completion of your program?
- Do you offer job-placement services through your program?
- How much does your program cost, and is financial aid available?

QUESTIONS TO ASK ABOUT APPRENTICESHIPS

- How many hours a week can I expect to work? (You need a certain number of hours to finish an apprenticeship, so this is an important question.)
- What parts of the trade can I expect to learn in an apprenticeship with you? (There are many different angles to the plumbing industry, as you've read, so you want to make sure the apprenticeship in question offers what you're looking for.)
- Will your program help prepare me for licensing exams?
- What is the pay?

QUESTIONS TO ASK WHEN INTERVIEWING FOR A PLUMBING JOB

- Do you provide opportunities for continued learning?
- Do you pay for certification classes and tests?
- What is your benefits package? (This typically covers medical insurance, life insurance, vacation time or paid time off, and retirement benefits. By asking this one question about benefits, you'll get the answer to several more questions.)
- Does this position require overtime often?
- What is the salary? (Don't forget this all-important question!)

NAIL THAT INTERVIEW!

Being interviewed can feel stressful. But here are some great steps you can take to ensure your interview goes as well as it possibly can:

- Dress for success! You should wear clean, well-fitting clothes that are free from words or graphics that might be questionable.
- Spend some time researching the position and company. Find out who is interviewing you and what they do. The more background information you have about the company and the interviewer, the better placed you will be.
- Prepare some questions ahead of time. Almost every interview ends with the employer asking you whether you have any questions for them. Have a question or two prepared to ask the interviewer.
- Thank the interviewer for their time.
- Follow up with a thank-you note by email or even text afterward.

GLOSSARY

accreditation certification that a school has met a specific set of standards set by an external group that regulates such schools

alternative energy relating to energy other than traditional types of energy such as fossil fuels, or coal, gas, and oil. Alternative energy includes sustainable energy such as solar and wind power

apprenticeship a position in which a person works for lower wages while learning a trade from a skilled professional

Armed Services Vocational Aptitude Battery (ASVAB) a test given to military enlistees to determine their aptitude and help guide their placement in the military

artificial intelligence (AI) technology designed to imitate human thought

associate's degree a two-year degree awarded to students who have completed a particular course of study at a community college

bachelor's degree a degree awarded to students who have completed a particular four-year course of study at a college or university

basic training a period of training for all new military enlistees

benefits services provided by employers in addition to wages. May include benefits such as health insurance, life insurance, retirement packages, stock options, and paid time off work

blueprints guides, designs, and plans that help with construction

certification a designation that one has completed a course of study (and usually passed a test) and has acquired a certain body of knowledge required in a field

civilian a person who is not in the military

community college a college that offers various associate's degrees as well as courses that can transfer to a university if a student wishes to pursue a bachelor's degree

component an element or part of something

conjunction at the same time or alongside something else

conservation to keep hold of something

diagnostic a tool used to diagnose a problem, or figure out what is causing a problem

drought a period of time with little or no rainfall

environmentally conscious aware of the environment and the impact that actions have on it, with a concern to protect it

flammable easily catches fire

graywater wastewater that comes from sinks, washing machines, tubs, and showers—not from toilets

hazardous dangerous to health

health insurance medical coverage to help a person pay medical bills for preventative care or emergencies

hydrostatic relating to the pressure created by a liquid when it is not moving

infectious related to a disease that can be passed from one person to another

infrastructure the basic structures and facilities, such as roads and buildings, needed for a society to operate

licenses certificates that show you are legally allowed to do a job

lucrative capable of producing much profit

mandatory required, often legally required

Medicare a federal health insurance system for people over age 65 and some people with disabilities. Everyone must pay into Medicare through their employer taxes or through self-employment tax

nonpotable not safe to drink

patent a government license that says an invention may be produced by only the patent holder for a specified period of time

peers people of a similar age

potable safe to drink

robot a machine that can replicate human movements

self-employment tax a required tax for contractors or others who are self-employed that covers Medicare and Social Security taxes that normally are taken out of one's paycheck by one's employer

sensor a device that detects something and responds to it

Social Security a government program that provides money to people who are retired or disabled

soldering joining together two metal surfaces by heating and melting a filling, called the solder, which is positioned between the two metal surfaces to fix them together

student loan a specific type of loan taken out by a person to attend college, university, or trade school

sustainable able to be maintained at a certain rate to avoid depleting natural resources, conserving ecological balance

total compensation package the salary and benefits offered by an employer to an employee. It may include wages, insurance, stock options, bonuses, and more

trade school a school that offers training for a particular career

university an institute of higher learning where students can earn a bachelor's degree and often a master's degree or doctorate degree

virtual reality (VR) a computer-generated simulation that humans can interact with using special equipment such as a headset or goggles

vocational related to work, for example, a school offers classes to students to train them for a skilled job or a trade

wastewater water that was used in a home or business

welding heating two metal surfaces to high temperature then pressing them together to join them

workers' compensation a type of insurance that covers lost wages and medical costs for employees injured on a job

FIND OUT MORE

BOOKS

Given-Wilson, Rachel. *Your Future as a Plumber* (High Demand Careers). Rosen Publishing, 2020.

Mason, P.D. *Apprenticeship Career Planning for Teens: A Comprehensive Guide to Securing Apprenticeships in High Demand Industries Without Taking on Years of College Debt.* SugarDog Publishing, 2023.

Mason, P.D. *Skilled Trade Career Planning for Teens: The Handbook of Lucrative Skilled Trades & High Paying Occupations That Don't Require Expensive College Degrees.* SugarDog Publishing, 2023.

WEBSITES

Bureau of Labor Statistics (BLS)

Take a look at the BLS website to find out more about the role and outlook for plumbers:
https://www.bls.gov/ooh/construction-and-extraction/plumbers-pipefitters-and-steamfitters.htm

Exploring

Exploring is a site that offers information about a lot of different paths for your future. They have a dedicated portion for trades, but the entire site is worth looking around in case there are other areas you're thinking of pursuing. They have a training portal and an activity library, too:
www.exploring.org

Explore the Trades

Explore the Trades is a great site for those interested in the plumbing, HVAC, and electrical trades. It provides a wealth of information on many aspects of working in these trades:
www.explorethetrades.org

Women in Plumbing & Piping

If you're looking for information on women in the plumbing industry, this site is the place to go. The site is part of a nonprofit that offers memberships, but even if you don't join at this point, the site is worth exploring for information on scholarships for women going into the field:
www.womeninplumbandpipe.org

Publisher's note to educators and parents:
All the websites featured above have been carefully reviewed to ensure that they are suitable for students. However, many websites change often, and we cannot guarantee that a site's future contents will continue to meet our high standards of educational value. Please be advised that students should be closely monitored whenever they access the Internet.

INDEX

ABOUT THE AUTHOR

Cathleen Small has written many books for young people on a wide variety of topics. She hopes this book will show readers that there are many exciting job opportunities for people who are interested in working as a plumber, and that the information provided will help set them on their path toward a perfect practical career.